THE MINI ADVENTURES OF
DANNY AND THE DEPLOYER

OPERATION CARE PACKAGE

THE MINI ADVENTURES OF
DANNY AND THE DEPLOYER

OPERATION CARE PACKAGE

Advantage Books

JUANDA RUTH BRYANT

ILLUSTRATIONS BY MITZIE STONE

The Mini Adventures of Danny and the Deployer: Operation Care Package
 by Juanda Ruth Bryant
Copyright © 2019 by Juanda Ruth Bryant
All Rights Reserved.
ISBN: 978-1-59755-530-2

Published by: ADVANTAGE BOOKS™
                       www.advbookstore.com

This book and parts thereof may not be reproduced in any form, stored in a retrieval system or transmitted in any form by any means (electronic, mechanical, photocopy, recording or otherwise) without prior written permission of the author, except as provided by United States of America copyright law.

Illustrations by Mitzie Stone

First Printing: July 2019
19 20 21 22 23 24 25   10 9 8 7 6 5 4 3 2 1
Printed in the United States of America

"Danny, are you okay?" asked Maya, the Marine.

"No, Maya, my dad has deployed, and I miss him," said Danny.

"There has to be something we can do because my mom deployed too," said Ava the Airman.

Sam, the Sailor said, "Let's play tag!"

Carlos, the Coast Guard, said, "Tag, you're it!"

In class, the teacher had the students write letters to their deployed parents:

Dear Dad,

I miss you so much. You are the best Dad ever! Thank you for protecting and serving our country.

Be safe and drink lots of water.

Love,
Danny

Danny tells the Deployer, "I wrote a letter to Dad today at school."

The Deployer said, "you can send a care package too."

"What, you can talk?" asked Danny.

"I can talk to you," said the Deployer.

Danny asked, "What is a care package?"

The Deployer explained that a care package contains things a loved one needs or wants. "Classified" means it's a secret between you and the other person.

"I got it," Danny said. "Dad and I love baseball!"

They begin to dig in the toy chest and found the baseball and glove that he and Dad use to play catch.

He also found matching water bottles of their favorite baseball team and decides to send one to Dad.

The Deployer's star lights up with excitement.

Danny said, "I want to send this nice family picture of us."

The star on the Deployer's chest lights up again to let Danny know the picture on the wall is a good choice.

Danny asks, "Mom can you to take me to the store so that I can get Dad a surprise gift for Dad's Care Package?"

Mom says, "Yes, I would love to."

Danny says, "I can't wait to work on my surprise!"

Mom yells, "Is everything okay in there?"

Danny yells back," Yes, ma'am! It's classified!"

Danny tells the Deployer, "I have the family picture, baseball, glove, water bottle, letter to Dad, Mom's letter to Dad, and the surprise in the box."

The Deployer says, "Let's put the address on the package, and then you're good to go."

From: Danny
2424 Battalion Drive
Fort Hood, Texas

To: Dad
123rd Transportation Company
APO, AE 09876

Mom says, "Danny here's the money to mail your care package. Your friends are outside waiting for you."

"Thanks, mom," said Danny.
As Danny and the Deployer walk to the post office, the Deployer's star beams with joy.

The surprise is a wristwatch! Danny's message on the watch said, "I love you, Dad," with Butch in the background barking.

This message made Dad smile so big and bright, just like the star on the Deployer's chest.

For more information contact:

Juanda Ruth Bryant
C/O Advantage Books
P.O. Box 160847
Altamonte Springs, FL 32716

info@advbooks.com

Also available:
The Mini Adventures of Danny and the Deployer (Book One)
ISBN: 978-1-59755-4336

To purchase additional copies of this book visit our bookstore website at: www.advbookstore.com

Longwood, Florida, USA
"we bring dreams to life"™
www.advbookstore.com

www.ingramcontent.com/pod-product-compliance
Lightning Source LLC
Chambersburg PA
CBHW081352040426
42450CB00015B/3407